# When I surrender to my kids

Navneet K Dhaliwal

# Table of Contents

## Introduction – Chapter 1

*Motherhood didn't just change my life it changed me. I spent years believing I was the one meant to guide, teach, and shape my children, never realizing that they had come into my world carrying lessons of their own. Their innocence, honesty, and raw emotions became a mirror reflecting everything I had forgotten about myself. In their presence, I began to see the parts of me I had buried beneath responsibility and fear. This chapter marks the moment I woke up to a truth I never expected: my children were not just looking to me for direction they were quietly leading me back to my own forgotten self.*

# Chapter 1

# The Awakening: When My Children Became My Teachers

I once believed motherhood meant guiding, shaping, and teaching my children. I thought I was the one who carried the wisdom, the answers, and the responsibility of molding them into who they were meant to become. Like many parents, I assumed they arrived in this world as blank pages, waiting for me to write their story. I believed my role was to protect them from mistakes, to correct them when they were wrong, and to show them the right path forward.

But the longer I lived inside the experience of being their mother, the more that belief slowly began to fall apart.

My children were never blank pages. They were mirrors.

Mirrors that reflected parts of me I had long stopped seeing. Parts of me I had hidden, ignored, or pushed aside in the rush of life. Their presence didn't just bring joy and laughter into my days—it brought awareness. It revealed things about myself that I had quietly buried beneath years of responsibility, fear, expectations, and survival.

Their innocence was not fragile the way I once believed. It was powerful. It carried a clarity that adults often lose as they grow older. They saw the world without the filters of doubt, shame, or judgment that I had slowly collected over the years. The way they spoke, the way they questioned things, the way they expressed their emotions it all carried a kind of truth that was both beautiful and confronting.

Sometimes their honesty caught me off guard.

Not because they were wrong, but because they were right in ways I wasn't ready to admit.

Their emotions were never the problem. They cried when they were hurt, laughed when they felt joy, and expressed frustration when something didn't feel fair. They didn't hide what they felt. They didn't pretend to be stronger than they were. They simply lived in their truth.

Watching them made me realize how much of myself I had silenced over the years.

There were moments when their behavior triggered something deep inside me. At first, I thought the frustration was about them. I believed they were being difficult, stubborn, or challenging. But slowly, painfully, I began to understand something much deeper.

It was never about them.

When impatience rose inside me, it was because I had never learned how to sit with my own discomfort. When I felt the urge to control their choices, it wasn't always about guiding them—it was often about trying to quiet the fear inside me. And when their emotions overwhelmed me, it was usually because I had spent years learning to suppress my own.

My children were unknowingly pointing toward every unhealed part of me.

And that realization was not easy.

It was uncomfortable to see how often I reacted instead of understanding. It was painful to recognize how many patterns I had carried from my own upbringing without even questioning them. But within that discomfort was also something incredibly powerful.

It was an invitation.

An invitation to look inward instead of outward.

Children do not enter this world empty. They come with intuition, curiosity, and a natural connection to who they are. They trust their feelings. They follow their instincts. They speak their truth without worrying about how the world might judge them.

They arrive whole.

And somewhere along the journey of becoming an adult, I had forgotten that I arrived whole too.

Before life layered expectations on my shoulders. Before responsibilities shaped my decisions. Before fears, disappointments, and the pressure to be "perfect" slowly pulled me away from the girl I once was.

There was a time when I moved through life with the same freedom my children now carried. A time when my imagination was alive, when my emotions were allowed to exist without shame, and when I trusted the quiet voice inside me that always knew the right direction.

But over the years, that voice became quieter.

Responsibilities replaced curiosity. Survival replaced joy. And slowly, without even realizing it, I drifted further away from my authentic self.

My children helped me see that.

Their questions made me pause and think about things I had long accepted without reflection. Their observations challenged beliefs I had inherited from others. Their presence reminded me of a simpler way of being one that was honest, open, and deeply connected to the heart.

Sometimes the mirror they held up to me was difficult to face.

It showed me my impatience, my fears, and the places where I had lost connection with myself. But it also showed me something else something hopeful.

It showed me that it wasn't too late to return.

Every day, through their laughter, their struggles, their curiosity, and their honesty, my children gently guided me back toward parts of myself I thought were gone forever. Not through lessons they intentionally taught, but through the simple way they lived their lives.

They reminded me that growth doesn't stop when we become parents.

In many ways, that is when it truly begins.

The moment I realized this was the moment everything shifted inside me. I stopped trying so hard to control every outcome. I stopped believing that my role was only to teach. Instead, I began to listen more carefully to their words, their feelings, and the wisdom hidden within their perspective.

I began to understand that motherhood was not just about raising children.

It was about raising myself too.

Healing the parts of me that needed compassion. Rediscovering the courage to live authentically. Learning to grow alongside the very souls I believed I was meant to guide.

My children were never here simply to be shaped by me.

They were here to shape me as well.

And in that realization, I found the true beginning of my journey. Not as the perfect parent who had all the answers, but as a human being willing to learn, to grow, and to be transformed by the beautiful, honest souls who had entered my life.

This was my awakening.

The moment I stopped trying to be only the teacher and finally allowed myself to become the student.

# Write about your Reflection

# Introduction – Chapter 2

*Sometimes the greatest changes in our lives do not come through force or determination, but through letting go. As a parent, I once believed that my responsibility was to guide every step of my children's journey, to protect them from mistakes, and to shape their future with careful control. But slowly, life began to show me something different. It revealed that love is not always about holding tighter it is often about learning when to loosen our grip. This chapter explores the quiet but powerful shift that happened when I began to understand that true motherhood was not about control, but about surrender.*

# Chapter 2

## The Journey of Surrender

There was a moment in my life that quietly changed everything. It didn't arrive with noise or drama, and no one around me noticed it happening. It was a simple realization that slowly settled into my heart like a truth I had been resisting for years. I began to understand that I was not here to control my children. I was here to learn how to surrender.

For a long time, I believed that being a good mother meant directing every step of my children's path. I thought it was my duty to guide their choices, correct their mistakes, and make sure they followed the "right" road in life. I carried the silent pressure of believing that their future depended entirely on how well I managed their journey. But over time, I started to see that this belief came from fear rather than love.

Surrender did not mean giving up on my responsibilities as a parent. It did not mean becoming careless or passive. Instead, it meant releasing the illusion that I had to control every outcome. It meant trusting that my children came into this world with their own inner wisdom, their own purpose, and their own path to discover.

Their souls carried a roadmap that existed long before I tried to design one for them.

Watching my children move through the world slowly opened my eyes to this truth. They approached life with a natural sense of alignment that I had somehow lost along the way. They trusted their intuition without questioning it. When something felt right, they followed it. When something felt wrong, they expressed it honestly. They laughed freely, cried openly, and allowed their emotions to exist without shame.

They didn't worry about how others might judge them. They didn't feel the need to hide their excitement, their curiosity, or their vulnerability. They simply lived in the truth of who they were.

And as I watched them, I realized how far I had drifted from that way of living.

Somewhere during my own childhood and adulthood, I had learned to silence parts of myself. I had been taught to shrink my voice when it felt too strong, to ignore my desires when they didn't match other people's expectations, and to follow rules designed to keep everyone else comfortable. Slowly, without even realizing it, I had built a version of myself that was shaped by fear and responsibility rather than authenticity.

My children unknowingly began to break those patterns open.

At first, I tried to guide them the way I had been guided. I corrected their behavior, questioned their choices, and worried about how their actions might affect their future. But the more I tried to "fix" them, the more I felt an uncomfortable tension inside myself. Something didn't feel right.

Then one day, I stopped trying to change them and started truly observing them.

That shift changed everything.

Instead of seeing children who needed constant direction, I began to see something deeper. I saw courage in their honesty. I saw wisdom in their instincts. I saw freedom in the way they expressed themselves without fear of judgment. And most surprisingly, I began to see a reflection of myself—not the adult I had become, but the child I once was.

The child who had once been curious, expressive, and unafraid to feel deeply.

That realization softened something inside me.

I began to understand that surrender was not weakness. It was trust. It was allowing space for my children to grow into who they were meant to be instead of forcing them into who I thought they should become. It was choosing presence over control, and connection over perfection.

Gradually, I began to release the pressure I had placed on myself.

I surrendered the need to always be right.

I surrendered the belief that I had to know every answer.

I surrendered the habit of leading from fear.

I surrendered the urge to hide my emotions or pretend I had everything figured out.

And something unexpected began to happen in that space.

Peace slowly entered my life.

Not the temporary calm that comes from things going perfectly, but a deeper kind of peace the kind that appears when you stop fighting the natural flow of life. It felt like finally allowing myself to float after years of exhausting effort to swim against a powerful current.

I realized my children did not need a perfect mother.

They needed a present one.

They needed a mother who could listen without immediately correcting, who could breathe through difficult moments, and who could trust that growth sometimes comes through experience rather than control. They needed a mother who could truly see them, not as projects to manage, but as souls unfolding in their own unique way.

This chapter of my life was not really about giving my children freedom.

It was about giving myself permission to let go.

And in doing so, I discovered something profound: everything I once feared losing was never mine to control in the first place. Letting go did not weaken the bond between us it deepened it. Through surrender, I found a quieter, gentler form of motherhood, one rooted not in fear or authority, but in trust, presence, and love.

# Write about your Reflection

## Introduction – Chapter 3

*There comes a point in motherhood when you realize your children are not just watching you they are reflecting you. They reflect your love, yes, but also your fears, your wounds, and the parts of yourself you've learned to hide from the world. In their presence, nothing stays buried for long. Their honesty, their purity, and their emotional clarity illuminate everything you thought you had outgrown or forgotten. This chapter is the moment I understood that my children were not exposing my flaws to shame me, but to help me heal the parts of myself I had abandoned. Through them, I learned that light and shadow walk together and both are needed for true transformation.*

# Chapter 3

# Light and Shadow: How My Children Helped Me Heal Myself

Children carry a kind of purity that adults spend years trying to reclaim. Their light is raw, bright, and unapologetically honest. It is a light that doesn't soften itself for anyone, and that light has a way of revealing everything you've tried to bury. My children never hurt me they revealed me. With every question I didn't want to answer, every moment they reacted to my unspoken stress rather than the words leaving my mouth, every time they pushed against rules that didn't feel fair, every time they responded to emotions I thought I had hidden... they were showing me the parts of myself I had long ignored.

They were showing me my shadow.

Not the darkness I feared was inside me, but the pieces I had pushed away:

the fear I had never dealt with,
the insecurities I pretended didn't exist,
the guilt I carried without knowing why,
the wounds I had collected over years,
the beliefs handed down from generations before me.

They didn't judge me for these shadows. They didn't shame me. They simply held up a mirror, shining their unfiltered light directly into the places I didn't want to confront.

Children don't operate from ego. They operate from truth.

And truth has a way of cracking you open gently, painfully, beautifully all at once.

My daughter's deep sensitivity exposed the ways I had learned to numb my own emotions to appear strong. Her tears reminded me of the ones I never let myself shed. My son's unwavering confidence challenged the parts of me that never felt worthy of taking up space. The way they questioned everything made me realize how much I had stopped questioning. Their presence alone showed me how long I had been disconnected from my own spirit, my own voice, my own needs.

Their light wasn't meant to blind me. It was meant to guide me.

But here's the thing about light: when it shines into a dark room, you finally see what has been hiding there all along. In the brightness of their presence, I began to see the truth I had avoided for years. I saw how many old wounds were still shaping my reactions. I saw how much of my frustration had nothing to do with them and everything to do with me. I saw how my impatience was not their fault, but the weight of emotions I still carried. I saw how my fears were not about their future, but were echoes from my own past that I had never healed.

My children weren't breaking me.

They were healing me.

Not with easy moments, but with honest ones the kind that forced me to slow down, to breathe deeper, to question my beliefs, to unlearn the patterns that no longer served me, and to grow into a version of myself that felt more real than ever before.

Motherhood didn't weaken me.

It peeled away everything I had built on fear, survival, and self-forgetting.

It stripped me back to the truth of who I was before the world told me who I should be.

Through my children, I learned emotional honesty.

I learned presence.

I learned that love is not just warmth sometimes it is truth, and sometimes it is reflection.

And somewhere along the way, something within me shifted.

Their light helped me stop running from my own shadow.

I learned to embrace both because both were part of my healing, part of my becoming, and part of the mother and woman I was always meant to be.

# Write about your Reflection

## Introduction – Chapter 4

*Many of us grow up believing that the way we were raised is simply the way parenting is supposed to be. We inherit rules, expectations, and beliefs about discipline without ever questioning where they came from or whether they truly nurture the hearts of our children. But when I became a mother, I began to see that there was a deeper way to raise a child—one rooted not in authority or fear, but in awareness, empathy, and connection. This chapter explores the powerful shift between traditional parenting and conscious parenting, and how my children gently led me to question everything I once believed about what it meant to be a "good parent."*

# Chapter 4

# Conscious Parenting vs. Traditional Parenting

I grew up in a world where parenting often meant control, correction, and unquestioned authority. Adults were seen as the ones who always knew best, and children were expected to obey without hesitation. Feelings were rarely explored, and emotions were often treated as inconveniences rather than signals of something deeper. Respect was measured by silence, and good behavior meant doing exactly what you were told.

For many families, this was simply the way things were done. It was the model passed down from generation to generation, rarely questioned because it was all anyone knew. I grew up believing that this structure was necessary, that discipline meant strictness, and that strong parenting required maintaining control at all times.

But becoming a mother slowly began to challenge those beliefs.

As I watched my children grow, I began to notice something important: beneath every behavior was an emotion, and beneath every emotion was a need. Their reactions were not random acts of defiance or stubbornness. They were expressions of feelings they didn't yet have the words to explain.

That realization began to shift the way I saw parenting.

Traditional parenting focuses heavily on behavior. When a child acts out, the goal is often to correct the action as quickly as possible. The question becomes, How do we stop this behavior? Rules are enforced, consequences are given, and the expectation is simple—children must learn to obey.

Conscious parenting asks a different question.

Instead of focusing only on what the child is doing, it asks why. Why are they upset? Why are they reacting this way? What emotion are they trying to communicate? And sometimes, the most uncomfortable question of all: What inside me is being triggered by this moment?

Traditional parenting often sounds like this:

"Do as I say."

"Because I'm the parent."

"Don't talk back."

"Stop crying."

These phrases are familiar to many of us because they were spoken to us growing up. They were not always said with cruelty— often they came from parents who were doing the best they could with what they had learned.

But conscious parenting begins with curiosity instead of authority. It asks deeper questions:

What are they feeling right now?

What do they need that they cannot yet express?

Why is this situation affecting me so strongly?

How can I respond with understanding instead of power?

One approach raises children who follow rules out of fear or obligation.

The other raises children who understand themselves.

For a long time, I believed that strictness was a sign of strength. I believed that quiet children were respectful children. I believed that good behavior meant I was doing my job well as a parent.

But over time, I began to see that silence was not always respect. Sometimes it was fear of disappointing, fear of punishment, fear of being misunderstood. And fear does not build confidence or emotional health. It simply teaches a child to hide parts of themselves.

I recognized something painful in that realization: the same patterns that had shaped my childhood had also shaped me as an adult. They had taught me to question my own voice, to doubt my feelings, and to prioritize pleasing others over understanding myself.

My children were showing me another way.

Through their honesty, their emotions, and their need for connection, they gently pushed me to shift my perspective. They showed me that parenting is not about controlling children—it is about guiding them while staying connected to their emotional world.

When I began listening instead of immediately reacting, something changed between us. When I validated their feelings instead of dismissing them, they felt safe enough to open up. When I explained things instead of simply commanding obedience, they began to trust me more deeply.

And perhaps most importantly, when I learned to regulate my own emotions taking a breath before responding, staying calm in moments of chaos they naturally began to mirror that calmness themselves.

Children do not need a dictator in their lives.

They need a guide—someone who models emotional maturity, empathy, and self-awareness. Someone who shows them that emotions are not problems to be silenced, but signals to be understood.

Traditional parenting often asks children to shrink themselves in order to fit expectations.

Conscious parenting asks the parent to grow.

Traditional parenting can unintentionally break a child's spirit, teaching them that obedience matters more than authenticity.

Conscious parenting nurtures that spirit, helping it grow strong enough to navigate the world with confidence and compassion.

Traditional parenting suppresses the child.

Conscious parenting transforms the parent.

Looking back now, I realize something that once felt difficult to admit: my children were never the problem. They were simply asking for something I had not yet learned how to give—an emotionally present and aware mother.

Learning to become that mother has been one of the most humbling journeys of my life. It has required patience, reflection, and a willingness to unlearn many of the beliefs I once held so tightly.

But in that process, something beautiful has happened.

As I learned to parent more consciously, I didn't just help my children grow.

I grew alongside them.

# Write about your Reflection

35

## Introduction – Chapter 5

*There comes a moment in parenthood when you look at your child and realize they are not simply growing they are becoming. Not becoming who you want them to be, but who they were always meant to be. It's a humbling moment, a sacred one, because it forces you to release the illusion that their future rests in your hands alone. This chapter is about that realization the moment I understood that my children were not here for me to shape, but for me to support. They arrived with their own inner compass, their own direction, their own soul roadmap. My role was never to create their path... only to walk beside them as they remembered it.*

# Chapter 5

# The Soul Roadmap

I once believed it was my responsibility to build my children's future to choose their interests, guide their steps, and protect them by shaping a life that was practical, stable, and safe. That belief was rooted in what many of us were taught growing up: a good parent knows best. A good parent decides what's right. A good parent directs, corrects, and prepares the child for the world.

But as I watched my children grow, something inside me shifted. I began to see a truth I had never considered before, a truth that felt both gentle and powerful: my children did not come here empty. They arrived with something sacred a soul roadmap, already imprinted with purpose, intuition, and a direction uniquely their own.

They were not blank slates waiting for me to write upon them. They were souls carrying wisdom, memories, and a journey that existed long before I ever became their mother. And every time I tried to steer them away from that inner knowing, I could feel the resistance in their energy.

Whenever I pushed them toward something "practical," their spirit pulled back.

Whenever I redirected them from what lit them up, their light dimmed.

Whenever I imposed choices rooted in my own fear fear of failure, fear of judgment, fear of uncertainty their joy flickered, even if only for a moment.

Children know.
Long before they can explain it in words, they know.

They know what feels right in their bodies.
They know what aligns with their spirit.
They know what sparks their passion, what expands their imagination, what draws their curiosity.

It is we the adults who forget.

We forget because we were told to "grow up" and "be realistic."

We forget because our dreams were dismissed as childish fantasies.

We forget because we were taught to trade what we love for what the world considers responsible.

My children reminded me that passion is responsibility to your inner truth, your inner joy, your inner calling.

Their roadmap was never mine to redraw.
It was mine to respect.
To protect.
To honor.

When my daughter danced, she wasn't simply moving her body she was remembering a piece of her soul, something ancient and familiar.

When my son questioned everything, he wasn't being difficult he was following a curiosity that would one day shape the man he was meant to become.

I realized my role was not to carve out their future.

My role was to remove the obstacles so they could walk freely into it.

To listen deeply when they spoke.
To observe gently when they didn't.
To trust their instincts even when they didn't align with my fears.
To let their interests evolve, to let their passions shift, to let their identity grow as they grew.

Their soul roadmap was not a straight, clean path.
It was fluid, alive, intuitive.
It changed with seasons, experiences, emotions, and stages of life.

Instead of leading from ahead or pushing from behind I learned to walk beside them.
Not to control.

Not to force.
Not to shape.

But to support.

Parenthood is not ownership it is stewardship of something divine.

Our children come *through* us,
but they do not belong *to* us.
They belong to their purpose, their spirit, their own becoming.

And when I finally accepted that truth, motherhood became lighter not because it suddenly got easier, but because I stopped trying to carry a responsibility that was never mine. I understood something profound:

I was never meant to write their story.
I was only meant to help them remember it.

# Write about your Reflection

# Introduction – Chapter 6

*Sometimes a child enters your life not only to be loved and protected, but to remind you of the person you once were. Their presence awakens memories, emotions, and forgotten parts of your spirit that you buried long ago while trying to fit into the world. My daughter became that mirror for me. In her creativity, her sensitivity, and her fearless way of expressing herself, I began to see the pieces of my own soul that I had quietly set aside. This chapter is about the powerful realization that while I was raising my daughter, she was also helping me rediscover myself.*

# Chapter 6

# My Daughter: The Mirror of My Forgotten Gifts

My daughter did not simply enter my life as my child. She entered as a reflection a living reminder of everything I had once been before life slowly taught me to hide parts of myself. From the very beginning, there was something about her presence that felt both beautiful and confronting. Her creativity, her softness, her imagination, her boldness, and her deep sensitivity flowed through her so naturally. These qualities seemed effortless for her, yet they stirred something deep inside me.

Because the truth was, those same qualities had once lived inside me too.

Somewhere along the journey of growing up, I had learned to push them down. I muted my colors so I could fit in more easily with the world around me. I dimmed my light because it felt safer than standing out. I hid my gifts because I had been taught that creativity and imagination were not practical, that dreams needed to be replaced with responsibilities.

Over time, those parts of me slowly became quiet.

But when my daughter arrived, something extraordinary happened. Without trying, without even knowing it, she began to reopen the doors I had closed long ago.

When she danced freely around the room, moving without hesitation or self-consciousness, I remembered the way my body once moved before I learned to worry about how others might see me. When she sang loudly and fearlessly, I remembered a younger version of myself who once expressed joy without holding back. When she sat on the floor creating drawings, paintings, and entire worlds out of scraps of paper, I remembered the little girl inside me who used to dream endlessly without asking for permission.

She never tried to teach me anything.

She simply existed fully, honestly, beautifully and her very being awakened something inside me that had been asleep for years.

Her emotions were just as powerful as her creativity. She felt everything deeply and expressed it openly, without apology. Joy, sadness, excitement, frustration she allowed each emotion to move through her naturally.

Watching her was both inspiring and uncomfortable at times.

Because I realized how much of my own emotional world I had learned to suppress. I had been taught that strength meant staying quiet, staying composed, and hiding anything that might appear too vulnerable.

But my daughter didn't live that way.

When she cried, her tears were honest and raw. In those moments, I saw the tears I had never allowed myself to shed. When she laughed from deep within her belly, her laughter filled the room with a joy that felt almost contagious. It reminded me of a kind of happiness I had forgotten how to access.

And when she asked her endless questions about life, about the world, about things that adults often overlook, I realized how long it had been since I had truly questioned anything myself.

She was everything I had forgotten I once was.

Instead of trying to change her or quiet the parts of her that seemed "too much," I slowly began to understand that my role was different. I was not here to shrink her spirit the way mine had once been shrunk. I was here to protect the parts of her that the world might one day try to take away.

I no longer wanted her to quiet down.

I wanted her to expand.

I no longer wanted her to be "strong" by suppressing her emotions.

I wanted her to feel everything deeply and honestly, because emotions are not weaknesses they are signals of a soul that is alive.

And I no longer wanted her to simply fit in.

I wanted her to shine.

Because somewhere along the way, I realized something profound: as I nurtured her growth, I was also healing myself.

Her light illuminated corners of my soul that had gathered dust over the years. Her boldness reminded me of dreams I had once tucked away because they seemed unrealistic. Her innocence helped me notice the beauty in everyday moments that adulthood had taught me to overlook.

My daughter was not only a child living in my home.

She was a guide.

A gentle healer.

A living reminder of the creative, sensitive, intuitive soul I had once been before the world convinced me to become smaller.

Through her, I began reconnecting with my creativity again. I began allowing my softness to exist without shame. I started listening to my intuition instead of ignoring it. I started remembering my truth.

Interestingly, the parts of her that sometimes frustrated me the most were often the parts of myself that still needed healing. Her intensity reflected emotions I had buried. Her independence challenged the control I sometimes clung to out of fear.

But the parts of her that inspired me her imagination, her courage to express herself, her deep emotional awareness were the parts of me that had been quietly waiting to be reborn.

Motherhood did not just give me a daughter.

It gave me a mirror one that helped me see myself more clearly than I had in years. And through loving and protecting the beautiful spirit of my daughter, I slowly began to reclaim the forgotten gifts that had always been mine.

# Write about your Reflection

## Introduction – Chapter 7

*Some children enter our lives not only to be nurtured, but to awaken something within us that we thought was lost. My son came into my world with a quiet, steady energy that demanded attention not through noise or drama, but through presence, curiosity, and an innate wisdom beyond his years. While my daughter helped me reclaim my creativity and softness, my son guided me back to my strength, my courage, and the parts of myself I had buried beneath responsibility and fear. This chapter is about the profound way he mirrored my own power, showing me that true strength is not control or force it is anchored, connected, and deeply present.*

# Chapter 7
# My Son: The Guide Who Led Me Back to Myself

My son entered my life with a presence that was different from anything I had experienced before. His energy was steady, grounding, and quietly bold, with a wisdom that seemed far beyond his years. Where my daughter awakened my creativity and reminded me of the parts of me that could dream freely, my son awakened a strength I had long forgotten a strength that did not come from control or authority, but from clarity, courage, and unwavering presence.

He had a way of seeing me that no one else could not my words, not my gestures, not the mask I had learned to wear but me. The parts of myself I had buried beneath expectations, responsibilities, and fear. When I felt overwhelmed, he sensed it immediately. When self-doubt crept in, he looked at me as if I could do anything. When I raised my voice out of fear rather than anger, he wasn't intimidated; he was curious. He wanted to understand why.

His questions were never meant to challenge my authority. They were meant to reveal truth my truth, his truth, the shared truth of our connection. He taught me that respect is not earned through obedience, but through understanding. And if I wanted him to truly hear me, I had to learn how to truly see him.

Through him, I began to recognize the parts of myself I had long ignored: my courage, my clarity, my ability to stand firm without hardening my heart. When he stood up for himself, he showed me where I had lost my own voice. When he questioned injustice, he reminded me of the times I accepted less than I deserved. When he expressed anger, he revealed the anger within me I had never processed. When he tested boundaries, he revealed where my own boundaries had never existed.

He was not defiant. He was honest. And that honesty forced me to examine the walls I had built to protect myself. He didn't need me to be perfect; he needed me to be present. To regulate myself before attempting to regulate him. To breathe before reacting. To explain instead of command. To lead with connection instead of fear.

My son taught me emotional strength the kind of strength that remains soft, even when life becomes hard. He reminded me that a strong mother is not one who controls, but one who stays anchored while allowing her children to unfold in their own way. He showed me that sensitivity and strength are not opposites they are partners.

In his confidence, I rediscovered my own.
In his questions, I remembered my curiosity.
In his courage, I reclaimed the bravery I once buried.
In his independence, I realized the importance of trusting not just him, but myself.

He guided me back to the version of me I had forgotten the version unafraid to speak up, to choose differently, to protect what mattered, and to stand firmly in her truth without apology.

My son didn't just grow under my care. I grew under his presence. He was not simply my child; he became my compass, my grounding force, and the living reminder that true strength is not loud or harsh it is steady, patient, and deeply connected.

# Write about your Reflection

53

# Introduction – Chapter 8

*Motherhood has a way of holding up a mirror, reflecting not just our love, but the fears, judgments, and old patterns we thought we had buried. The very act of raising children can feel like a gentle yet relentless detox pulling out the beliefs and programming that no longer serve us, forcing us to confront the ways we've carried fear, guilt, and shame across generations. This chapter explores that journey, the inner work that motherhood demanded of me, and the way my children guided me to release what wasn't mine so I could become the parent they truly needed.*

# Chapter 8

# The Detox: Removing Fear, Judgment, and Old Programming

Motherhood has a way of exposing everything you carry not just the love, but also the fear. Not just the dreams, but the wounds. And as my children grew, I realized something profound: I wasn't just raising them. I was detoxing myself.

Not a physical detox, but a detox of my beliefs.
A detox of the old programming that had shaped me.
A detox of the fear that had been passed down through generations.
A detox of the judgment I had learned to place on myself long before I ever became a mother.

It wasn't that my children were triggering me they were revealing what needed to be released. Every reaction, every moment of tension, every emotion reflected back something buried inside me. They showed me the depth of my own fears:

Fear of failing.
Fear of being judged.
Fear of not being enough.
Fear of messing everything up.
Fear of repeating patterns I had promised myself I would break.

And then the truth of motherhood hit me with clarity: children absorb more than our words they absorb our unhealed fears.

When I was anxious, they tightened. When I doubted myself, they hesitated. When I rushed, they felt unsafe. When I judged myself, they felt judged too.

It wasn't about perfection. It was about presence.

I realized I had to detox myself from all that no longer served the parent I wanted to be:

- The critical voice in my head whispering, "You're not doing enough."
- The pressure to parent according to society's expectations.
- The urge to compare my children to others.
- The inherited guilt from my own childhood.
- The belief that love must look or feel a certain way.

Children do not need a perfect parent. They need a healed parent or at least a parent committed to the process of healing.

And healing didn't happen overnight. It happened in moments.

Moments when I chose patience over frustration.
Moments when I paused instead of reacting.
Moments when I apologized instead of exerting control.
Moments when I allowed myself to cry instead of holding everything in.
Moments when I let them express themselves fully, without shutting them down.

Every conscious choice softened something in me.
Every act of awareness dissolved a little more fear.
Every deep breath broke another chain of patterns passed down through generations.

Slowly, I began letting go:

- Of outdated expectations.
- Of rigid beliefs that no longer served anyone.
- Of rules that had never made sense.
- Of shame that was never truly mine.
- Of voices that did not belong to me.
- Of the mother I thought I had to be.

And in that release, I finally became the mother my children truly needed.

The detox wasn't about changing them. It was about transforming me, so they could grow without carrying what I had inherited.

My children didn't need me to be perfect or fully healed to love me. But they guided me toward healing so I could learn to love myself fully.

And that is the quiet miracle of motherhood the way it strips you down, clears out the old, and slowly rebuilds you into someone softer, stronger, and more authentic than you ever imagined possible.

# Write about your Reflection

# Introduction – Chapter 9

*Parenting is often misunderstood as shaping the child's future, steering every decision, and controlling outcomes. But the most profound lessons I've learned are about creating space, not control; about tending the soil instead of forcing the flower. This chapter explores the subtle yet transformative shift I experienced when I realized that my job was never to mold who my children become, but to craft an environment that nurtures their natural growth. It is in the safety, freedom, and trust we provide that children truly blossom and in that process, we learn to bloom ourselves.*

# Chapter 9

# Creating the Environment, Not the Outcome

One of the most important shifts in my motherhood journey came when I realized that my role was never to control who my children become. My responsibility was not to dictate their choices, force their steps, or ensure they turned out "right." My true role was to create an environment that allowed them to flourish, that supported them in becoming their authentic selves.

For years, I had believed that parenting meant shaping their future guiding every decision, steering every interest, and attempting to craft the person they would become. I thought success as a mother depended on the outcome. But the truth is much simpler and far more profound: a child becomes who they are meant to be when the environment around them nurtures their growth.

It is like a plant. You do not force a seed to grow by pulling at its leaves. You do not scold it for not blooming fast enough. You do not compare it to the plant next to it. You do not punish it for growing sideways or demand that it flowers before it has rooted. What you do is simple: you water it. You give it sunlight. You protect it from harsh winds. You give it space. You trust the process. You allow it to bloom in its own time.

Children are no different. They do not need pressure they need presence. They do not need control they need support. They do not need perfection they need safety. They do not need molding they need trust.

The moment I stopped focusing on shaping the "outcome," I shifted my attention to the environment I was creating. I focused on building spaces where my children could speak without fear, where their emotions were welcomed instead of dismissed, where mistakes were lessons instead of punishments, where their passions were nurtured rather than questioned, and where curiosity was celebrated instead of stifled.

I began noticing profound changes. My children opened up more freely. Their confidence grew. Their unique personalities unfolded naturally and beautifully. Their creativity expanded without limits. They became calmer, more connected, more aligned with their own inner truths. They thrived because they finally felt safe to grow at their own pace, in their own way.

As a parent, it is easy to panic when immediate results are not visible. But transformation often happens quietly, beneath the surface, like seeds breaking through the soil. One day, when you least expect it, the growth becomes undeniable.

My children did not need me to design their destiny. They needed me to protect the soil in which it would grow. The environment I cultivated shaped more than their childhood it shaped their emotional foundation, their sense of self-worth, and their inner voice.

And in creating that environment for them, I healed a part of myself as well. I finally understood what I had longed for in my own childhood: a place where I could grow, explore, and bloom without fear, without judgment, and without losing myself. By nurturing that for my children, I finally learned how to nurture it for myself too.

# Write about your Reflection

63

# Introduction – Chapter 10

*Motherhood is often described as love, sacrifice, and responsibility but those words barely scratch the surface. It is far deeper, far more sacred. Motherhood is a journey of the soul. It transforms a woman in ways that are quiet, profound, and sometimes painful. It awakens parts of you that have been hidden, softens parts hardened by life, and stretches your heart beyond anything you imagined possible. This chapter dives into the sacred and transformative power of motherhood the way it reshapes you while guiding your children, the way it asks you to grow, heal, and awaken alongside them.*

# Chapter 10
# The Sacred Role of a Mother

Motherhood is often spoken of in simple terms: love, sacrifice, and responsibility. But those words cannot capture the depth of the experience, the quiet, unseen transformation that unfolds when a woman steps into this sacred role. Motherhood is spiritual. It is soul work. It is a journey that reshapes you from the inside out, revealing parts of yourself you had forgotten and awakening strengths you never knew existed.

When I became a mother, I realized quickly that this role was not something I stepped into it was something that awakened within me. My instincts sharpened. My emotions deepened. My heart stretched in ways I never imagined possible. And with that awakening came a truth I wasn't prepared for: motherhood is not just about raising children it is about becoming the version of yourself they came to learn from.

The responsibility can feel overwhelming not the practical tasks of feeding, bathing, and teaching, but the weight of shaping a safe emotional home. A home where children can return not just physically, but mentally, spiritually, and energetically. Motherhood demanded more honesty than I had ever given myself. I could no longer hide behind old patterns. I could not ignore my wounds. I could not pretend to be someone I was not. Children feel everything. They respond not just to what you say, but to who you are in every moment.

And that truth forced me to evolve. Every fear I carried about being a "good mother" stemmed from the pressure to get it right, to perform perfectly, to never fail. Slowly, I learned that children don't need perfection. They need authenticity. They need warmth. They need presence. They need connection. They need a mother who is trying her hardest, not a mother who is flawless.

The sacredness of motherhood lies in the invisible, everyday moments: in the way you whisper encouragement when no one is watching; in the way you hold their trembling hand when the world feels too big; in the way you apologize when you've hurt them, showing that even adults make mistakes; in the way you protect their innocence while preparing them for life's harsh truths; in the way you hold space for their emotions, even when it awakens your own old wounds; in the way you guide them to navigate the world without losing themselves in it.

Pregnancy had tested me the fear, uncertainty, and vulnerability of carrying life inside me. But raising them tested me in ways that went far beyond the physical. It tested my soul.

Motherhood demanded emotional strength I had never had before. It required me to soften where I had hardened, to listen when I wanted to shout, to choose patience when every instinct screamed otherwise, to love even on days I felt empty, and to forgive even when my heart felt heavy.

Motherhood is not a role it is a calling. A sacred, invisible contract between souls. My children chose me, not because I would be perfect, but because I would grow with them, heal with them, and awaken with them. Motherhood is not about giving children the best version of life it is about giving them the best version of you. A version that evolves, softens, strengthens, and awakens over time.

It is in the quiet nights when I watch them sleep, their tiny chests rising and falling, that I feel the weight and beauty of this sacred role. In those moments, I realize that every tear, every worry, every sleepless night, every fear, and every sacrifice has been worth it. Motherhood does not make you smaller. It makes you vast. It expands the heart, stretches the soul, and calls forth a depth of love you never imagined existed.

Through motherhood, I have learned that the love I give is not just for them it is also for me. It teaches me patience I never knew I had, courage I had forgotten, resilience I thought I lacked, and grace I had not yet learned to offer myself. In guiding them, I am guided. In teaching them, I am taught. In loving them, I am reminded of the infinite capacity of the human heart.

Motherhood is not about being the perfect mother. It is about being fully present, fully human, fully open to growth, healing, and transformation. And in embracing that sacred journey, I have discovered a truth more profound than I could have imagined: that motherhood does not take from you it awakens you. It does not confine you it liberates you. It does not demand perfection it demands authenticity.

And in giving everything to them, they have given everything back to me. My children are mirrors, teachers, and guides, showing me the sacredness of life, the depth of love, and the limitless capacity of the heart. Through them, I have found myself again, and through them, I continue to grow into the mother I was always meant to be.

# Write about your Reflection

## Introduction – Chapter 11

*One of the hardest lessons in motherhood is learning to release control and let your children grow beyond the limits you once knew. We want to protect them, guide them, and keep them safe but the truth is, they are here to expand far beyond our comfort zones, to shine brighter than we ever imagined. This chapter explores the courage it takes to step back, to honor their unique path, and to celebrate the versions of themselves that may surpass even our wildest dreams.*

# Chapter 11
## Letting Them Be Bigger Than You

One of the most challenging truths I had to face as a mother was this: my children are not here to become smaller versions of me. They are here to become bigger, brighter, more expansive versions of themselves. For so long, I had unconsciously believed that my role was to guide them down the path I understood, the one that felt safe, familiar, and predictable. But children are not meant to live inside the boundaries of our comfort zones. They are here to explore, expand, and surpass them.

My children did not inherit my limits they inherited my light, and they came to make it shine brighter. But to honor that, I had to confront something uncomfortable: sometimes, a mother can become the ceiling that prevents her child from rising higher. Not out of malice, but out of fear. Fear that they might fail. Fear that the world might hurt them. Fear that they might outgrow us. Fear that they might discover a version of themselves we do not fully understand.

Growth does not come from staying small. Growth comes from reaching, exploring, wandering, falling, rising, and daring to dream. And to allow that, I had to release control. My role was no longer to mold them into something familiar or predictable it was to create the space for them to become something I had never seen before. I had to let them surpass me not in accolades or achievements, but in consciousness, in alignment, in being.

I had to let them:

- Think bigger than I ever did,
- Question more than I was allowed to,
- Feel more deeply than I learned to,
- Dream without shrinking,
- Speak without fear,
- Explore without apology.

Every time I caught myself trying to pull them back into "what made sense," I realized it wasn't their limitation it was mine. Their vision was wider. Their courage purer. Their intuition clearer. And instead of dimming it, I learned to protect it.

Letting my children be bigger than me meant embracing dreams that scared me. It meant supporting choices I could not always predict. It meant trusting their inner voice even when I did not fully understand it. It meant stepping back without disconnecting. Guiding without controlling. Watching without interfering. It meant knowing that the greatest gift I could give them was not the path I walked, but the wings I never had.

Children are not here to repeat our stories they are here to write their own. And if their stories take them farther, higher, braver, and deeper than I ever went, then I have done my job as a mother. Letting them be bigger than me did not diminish me it freed me. Free to grow with them, free to learn from them, free to evolve beside them.

Motherhood is not about raising children who follow our footsteps. It is about raising children who carve their own path and knowing that they were never meant to walk behind us, but in front of us, leading the way, illuminating the world in ways we could never imagine.

And in letting them rise, I discovered that my heart could expand far beyond what I thought was possible, because their courage taught me the true depth of love a love that does not bind, but lifts, not controls, but sets free.

# Write about your Reflection

# Introduction – Chapter 12

*Motherhood begins as something we give our love, our guidance, our time, our energy but its deepest magic is what it gives back. It returns to us the parts of ourselves we thought were lost, hidden, or forgotten. This chapter explores the sacred journey of becoming whole again through our children, of rediscovering the woman we were always meant to be, and of learning that motherhood is not just about raising them it is about reclaiming ourselves.*

# Chapter 12
# Becoming Whole Again

Motherhood began for me as a gift I thought I would give to my children my time, my love, my energy, my guidance. I imagined it as an act of giving, shaping, and nurturing. But somewhere along the journey, I realized a deeper truth: my children were giving me back to myself. Piece by piece. Moment by moment. Reflection by reflection. They were helping me stitch together the parts of me I had lost, forgotten, or hidden away.

Through their presence, I remembered who I once was before life taught me to shrink, before responsibilities hardened me, before fear silenced my voice. Their presence brought me home. Every time they dreamed without fear, I remembered the dreams I had abandoned. Every time they felt deeply, I confronted the emotions I had buried. Every time they stood in their truth, I saw the truths I had silenced. Every time they expressed pure joy, I felt joy I thought I had outgrown. They restored color to the gray corners of my life.

Motherhood did not break me it broke open the spaces within me that needed light. I began to reconnect with what made me feel alive: my creativity, my self-expression, my softness, my curiosity, my intuition. Not because I suddenly chose to explore these parts of myself, but because I witnessed them shining so brightly in my children. They became mirrors, reflecting not just the mother I had become, but the woman I had forgotten. And through these reflections, I found her again.

I learned to slow down. To breathe. To honor my body. To trust my instincts. To respect my emotions. To set boundaries. To say no when needed, and to say yes to what nourished my soul. I realized that becoming a whole mother required first becoming a whole woman not perfect, but whole. Whole enough to feel, whole enough to rest, whole enough to fail and try again. Whole enough to show up as myself, not as a version shaped by fear, duty, or expectation.

I stopped trying to fit into motherhood and allowed motherhood to fit into me. I stopped chasing the version of myself I thought I needed to be and embraced the woman I already was. My children did not need a mother with all the answers they needed a mother who was alive, present, authentic, and willing to grow.

Wholeness, I realized, was not perfection it was presence. Not control it was connection. Not knowing everything—it was being open to learning. Not losing myself in motherhood it was finding myself through it. Motherhood did not complete me it revealed me. It peeled back the layers I had accumulated over the years until I stood in the truth of who I had always been.

And now, standing here wiser, softer, and more aligned than I ever imagined, I understand the greatest gift my children have given me: not just love, not just purpose, but wholeness the return to the woman I was always meant to be.

They did not just teach me how to be a mother they taught me how to be fully, beautifully, and unapologetically myself again.

# Write about your Reflection

# Author's Reflection

My journey of motherhood taught me far more about myself and my soul's path than I ever expected. Through becoming a mother, I discovered many hidden parts of myself. It completely changed the way I think about relationships, parenting, and the deeper purpose of raising children.

Before I became pregnant, I had already been on a long journey of self-discovery. That journey gave me awareness, but it wasn't enough to fully illuminate the path ahead of me. Motherhood helped me expand that light. It showed me how to make that light brighter and stronger so it could guide not only me, but also my children.

During this process I realized something beautiful: I was becoming a mother, a child, and a student all at the same time. Parenting was not just about teaching my children. It was also about learning from them and growing alongside them.

Being a mother has been the most powerful experience of my life. Pregnancy itself carries both pain and beauty. There is discomfort, fear, and uncertainty, yet there is also pride and a deep sense of joy in knowing that you are bringing a new life into the world.

When I was pregnant, I had so many fears and questions. I wondered how to raise my child the right way, how to behave, how to feed them, and how to comfort them. The uncertainty begins even during pregnancy, when we do not truly know what is happening inside our bodies.

We wonder how the baby is growing, what they are feeling, and how they are being nourished. Sometimes the baby moves, and sometimes there is silence, and that silence can fill a mother's heart with worry. I often asked myself why the baby was moving so much one day and so little the next. Those questions can keep a mother awake at night.

I remember worrying whether my body was accepting the food I was eating or whether my baby was rejecting it. If the baby rejected it, how would they grow? How would they survive? These thoughts created fear within me, because all I wanted was to protect that little life growing inside me.

It is such a strange and powerful feeling to worry deeply about someone you have not even seen or met yet. Yet that is the nature of motherhood. The love begins long before the child arrives.

A mother goes through countless emotional and physical changes during this time. Carrying a life inside your womb transforms you. Suddenly there is responsibility, fear, hope, and love all growing together within you.

The journey of motherhood is truly a mixture of pain and pleasure. Through that journey I realized how important self-awareness is. When we become aware of ourselves, we understand our emotions and fears better, and that awareness allows us to grow.

Through my children, I grew spiritually and emotionally. Connecting with them helped me connect more deeply with myself. It helped me understand my role in their lives in a completely new way.

Sometimes children have a beautiful way of transforming us. They take the parts of ourselves that we once considered ugly or broken and help turn them into something beautiful. Their love has the power to heal wounds we didn't even realize we were carrying.

Children often shine a light on the darkest parts of us. When they arrive with strong, bright energy, they help us overcome our own darkness. They inspire us to become stronger and more whole so that we can create a safe and loving environment where their light can continue to grow.

When I conceived my son, I felt a powerful change within myself. My energy shifted, and I felt a sense of balance I had never experienced before. It felt as though a divine soul had entered my life, bringing a new kind of light with it.

I naturally began making different choices. I started eating more organic foods and choosing things that felt more natural and nourishing. I found myself eating foods I normally wouldn't choose, especially foods rich in protein and healthy fats.

At the time, I didn't fully understand why I was craving these things. But after my son was born, I realized that those choices were exactly what his growing body needed. It was as if his needs were guiding me from within.

Sometimes during pregnancy, we crave foods we never normally eat. Those cravings can feel strange, but they often come from the needs of the life growing inside us. I rarely ate fatty foods before, but during my pregnancy with my son, I felt drawn to them because his body needed that nourishment to grow strong.

Looking back, I realized that I was not fully in control of the process. Something greater was unfolding through me. I was simply a vessel preparing to bring a new soul into the world.

That realization taught me surrender. I allowed the process to unfold naturally, trusting that my body and my spirit were being guided in the right direction.

My second pregnancy felt completely different. I did not yet know that I was carrying a baby girl, but everything about my experience felt softer and lighter than before.

My emotions were gentler. I felt more sensitive and calm. I craved lighter foods, and my body felt more delicate and peaceful. I didn't understand the reason at the time, but looking back now, I can see that my body was adjusting to the different energy of the soul I was carrying.

I felt as though I had to become softer and more gentle so that I could hold that beautiful energy within me. Once again, I surrendered to the process and allowed my body and spirit to adapt.

After both pregnancies, I began to understand these differences more clearly. Certain foods I craved with my son are still foods he loves today. It feels as though he was asking for them even before he was born.

I believe that every child comes into the world with their own unique soul roadmap. If they are meant to do something special in life, the path to that purpose already exists within them.

As parents, we may not always understand that path, because it may be very different from the road we ourselves have walked. But our responsibility is not to control their journey. Our responsibility is to support them and give them the space to grow.

When we allow children that freedom, they develop their wings. Those wings grow stronger over time, allowing them to fly higher than we ever did.

They will face storms and strong winds along the way, but their connection to their soul's path will guide them through those challenges.

If children simply follow the exact path we give them, they may only reach the same place we reached. But they are the next generation. They are meant to go further than we did.

We should not limit them with our expectations or fears. They will discover their own gifts, and those gifts may have the power to change many lives.

When we try to control them or place them inside a box, we unintentionally make them dependent on us. Instead of growing freely, they remain tied to our decisions and our fears.

In the long run, this prevents both parents and children from truly becoming free. Children may spend their lives dealing with their parents' struggles rather than discovering their own purpose.

Eventually, they may become lost or exhausted from carrying burdens that were never meant to be theirs.

That is why it is so important not to pass our unresolved struggles to our children. Those challenges were given to us so that we could grow and find our own path toward healing and freedom.

The more we work on ourselves, the more we grow closer to our children. The more we heal, the more they flourish.

When we surrender to our own growth and light, our children naturally guide us toward a brighter future one where both they and we can grow together.

# To My Parents with Gratitude

Before I became a mother, I was a daughter. And before I could understand the depth of sacrifice, love, fear, and responsibility that comes with raising a child, my parents had already lived that journey for me. Today, as I walk the path of motherhood myself, I look back at my childhood with a deeper understanding and a heart full of gratitude. I am thankful to my parents for raising me the best way they knew how. They gave me strength, discipline, protection, and values that shaped the woman I am today. The world they grew up in was different. Parenting in their time was built on responsibility, survival, respect, and doing what they believed would prepare their children for a hard world. They may not have always expressed love in the same language that we speak today, but their love was present in every sacrifice they made. It was in the long days they worked, the worries they carried silently, the lessons they repeated again and again, and the boundaries they set to keep us safe. Because of them, I learned resilience. Because of them, I learned discipline. Because of them, I learned how to stand strong in life. Their parenting made me strong enough to face my own journey. Now, as I raise my own children in a different generation, I have discovered something new. Motherhood opened another door of awareness for me. While my parents gave me the roots that grounded me, my children are teaching me how to grow new branches. The world is changing, and so is parenting. What our parents gave us was what they believed was right for their time. What we give our children now must evolve with the new awareness we are discovering. My journey of motherhood did not make me reject the way I was raised. Instead, it helped me understand it more deeply. I now see that every generation learns something new. Our parents gave us strength to survive the world they knew. And now our children are guiding us to grow in a world that asks for more awareness, more connection, and more emotional understanding. So this book is not written against the way we were raised. It is written with gratitude for it. Because the strength my parents built inside me is exactly what allowed me to question, to grow, and to become the woman and mother I am today. To my parents thank you for raising me with the love, courage, and dedication you had. Your parenting gave me my foundation. And from that foundation, I am learning how to build something new for the next generation. With love and gratitude.